OUTSTANDING AFRICAN AMERICANS

GREAT AFRICAN AMERICANS IN

Jazz

CARLOTTA HACKER

Crabtree Publishing Company

Dedication

This series is dedicated to the African-American men and women who followed their dreams. With courage, faith, and hard work, they overcame obstacles in their lives and went on to excel in their fields. They set standards as some of the best Olympic athletes in the world. They brought innovation to film, jazz, and the arts, and the world is richer for their touch. They became leaders, and through their example encouraged hope and self-reliance. *Outstanding African Americans* is both an acknowledgment of and a tribute to these people.

Project Manager
Lauri Seidlitz

Production Manager
Amanda Howard

Editor
Virginia Mainprize

Copy Editor
Janice Parker

Design
Warren Clark

Layout
Chris Bowerman

Photograph Credits
Cover: Davis photo (Archive: Gerald Davis), Armstrong and McRae photos (Photofest); **Archive Photos:** pages 13 (Gerald Davis), 30, 43 (Frank Driggs Collection), 8, 29; **Canapress Photo Service:** page 28; **Charles L. Blockson Afro-American Collection, Temple University:** page 41; **Corbis-Bettmann:** pages 26 (Carole & Florence Reiff), 18, 23, 42, 45; **Frank Driggs/Corbis-Bettmann:** pages 36, 40; **Globe Photos:** pages 15 (Michael Ferguson), 20 (Christopher R. Harris), 55 (Adam Scull), 9, 21, 22; **Muse Records:** page 46; **Photofest:** pages 19 (Ed Peters), 4, 6, 12, 16, 49, 58, 61; **Reuters/Corbis-Bettmann:** page 10 (Greg Bos); **Schomburg Center for Research in Black Culture, New York Public Library:** pages 44 (Carl Van Vechten), 5, 11, 17, 25, 27, 35, 52; **UPI/Corbis-Bettmann:** pages 38 (Dave Boyer), 7, 14, 24, 33, 34, 37, 39; **Urban Archives, Temple University, Philadelphia, Pennsylvania:** pages 31 (James), 32.

Every reasonable effort has been made to trace ownership and to obtain permission to reprint copyright material. The publishers would be pleased to have any errors or omissions brought to their attention so that they may be corrected in subsequent printings.

Published by
Crabtree Publishing Company

350 Fifth Avenue,	360 York Road, R.R. 4	73 Lime Walk
Suite 3308	Niagara-on-the-Lake	Headington
New York, NY	Ontario, Canada	Oxford OX3 7AD
U.S.A. 10018	L0S 1J0	United Kingdom

Copyright © 1997 WEIGL EDUCATIONAL PUBLISHERS LIMITED. All rights reserved. No part of this publication may be reproduced, stored in a retrieval system or be transmitted in any form or by any means, electronic, mechanical, photocopying, recording, or otherwise, without the prior written permission of Weigl Educational Publishers Limited.

Cataloging-in-Publication Data

Hacker, Carlotta.
    Great African Americans in jazz / Carlotta Hacker.
        p.   cm. — (Outstanding African Americans)
    Includes index.
    Summary: Profiles of thirteen African-American jazz musicians, including Miles Davis, Duke Ellington, and Billie Holiday.
        ISBN 0-86505-818-0 (paper). — ISBN 0-86505-804-0 (RLB)
        1. Jazz musicians—United States—Biography—Juvenile literature. 2. Afro-American musicians—Biography—Juvenile literature.
    [1. Musicians. 2. Afro-Americans—Biography. 3. Jazz.]   I. Title.   II. Series.
    ML3929.H33 1997
    781.65'092'273—dc20
    [B]   96-41844
                                                                    CIP
                                                                 AC MN

Contents

For other great African Americans in jazz, see the book

GREAT AFRICAN AMERICANS IN MUSIC

Ella Fitzgerald • Sarah Vaughan…and others!

Louis Armstrong

Family: Married Daisy Parker, 1918, (divorced); married Lil Hardin, 1924, (divorced, 1938); married Alpha Smith, 1938, (divorced, 1942); married Lucille Wilson, 1942.

Awards: Grammy for Best Male Vocal Performance, 1964; Jazzmobile Award, 1967; Lifetime Achievement Award, National Academy of Recording Arts and Sciences (NARAS), 1972; "West End Blues" inducted into the NARAS Hall of Fame, 1974; Grand Master Award, Jazz Heritage Society, 1976; voted best trumpeter in many jazz magazine polls, including five times in *Metronome* magazine and five times in *Down Beat* magazine.

Personality Profile

Career: Trumpet player and singer.

Born: August 4, 1901, in New Orleans, Louisiana, to Willie and Mary Ann Armstrong.

Died: July 6, 1971, in Queens, New York.

Growing Up

Louis's parents were separated, and his mother was always short of cash. Louis sold papers and ran errands to help make ends meet. Every dime he could earn was a big help. When he was only nine years old, he sold buckets of coal from door-to-door. Louis first performed in public when he was about ten. He and his friends sang in the streets of New Orleans, Louisiana, earning a few cents to take home to their families.

Louis and his mother lived in Storyville, a tough district of New Orleans. It was an exciting place for a boy. Music from the dance halls and clubs spilled out onto the sidewalks. Often ragtime bands marched through the streets, playing their honky-tonk music. Louis and his friends would tag along behind the musicians. "I was brought up around music," he once said.

"Jazz and I grew up side by side."

Although Louis loved music, he had no chance to play it. His mother could not afford music lessons. He might never have become a famous jazz trumpet player if he had not become too excited one night when he was about twelve. During a New Year's Eve celebration, he fired a pistol into the air—and was arrested. "I was just a kid," he later recalled. "Oh, but I cried." This proved to be the turning point of his life. He was sent to a reform school, and there he learned to read music and play the cornet, an instrument similar to a trumpet.

Developing Skills

"Music's my language. On all those trips all over the world, maybe the musicians can't speak with you, but play 'Struttin' with Some Barbecue' and they'll know their parts and chime right in."

L ouis was thirteen when he left reform school. Taking odd jobs, he earned enough money to continue music lessons and buy a second-hand cornet. In the evenings, he went to local clubs to hear musicians. He was so eager to learn that the famous bandleader Joe "King" Oliver agreed to teach him. Soon Louis was playing so well that he was often asked to fill in with local bands.

For the next few years, Louis played with jazz bands on the Mississippi river boats and around New Orleans. Then he was asked by King Oliver to join his new Creole Jazz Band in Chicago. Louis made his first recording in 1923 with Oliver. His playing was attracting a lot of attention and so was his deep, gravelly singing voice.

In the mid-1920s, Louis switched from the cornet to the trumpet. Soon he was performing with a number of different bands. His trumpet playing was joyful, and he experimented as he played. He did not stick only to the Dixieland style but also played freely, setting jazz on a new path.

Louis was the first to record scat, a new type of singing that uses syllables instead of words. This happened during a recording session when he dropped his sheet music and could not remember the words. It sounded so good that other jazz singers copied the style. During this period, he teamed up with other musicians to make the "Hot Five" and "Hot Seven" recordings. These records greatly influenced the development of jazz.

In 1925, Louis formed his own band. His fame spread, and soon he became the leading jazz musician of the day. He was offered parts in Broadway shows and movies. By the 1950s, Louis was famous throughout the world. He visited Africa in 1956, and during the 1960s, he toured in countries as far away as Australia, Iceland, Japan, and Czechoslovakia. Everywhere he went he was greeted by adoring fans.

In 1964, he had his all-time greatest hit, "Hello Dolly," which replaced a Beatles album on the top of the record charts. During his career he made almost two thousand recordings, including "Mack the Knife," "Blueberry Hill," and "What a Wonderful World."

Louis sang in German during a 1959 appearance in the German film **The Night before the Premiere.**

Accomplishments

1922-24 Played in King Oliver's jazz band.

1923 Made first recording.

1925 Formed first band of his own, Louis Armstrong and His Hot Five.

1931 Appeared in *Ex-Flame*, his first of more than thirty movies.

1932 First European tour.

1956 First visit to Africa.

1963 Performed for President Kennedy.

1969 Appeared in *Hello Dolly*, a hit movie.

1972 Lifetime Achievement Award, NARAS.

1975 Program featuring his music toured the Soviet Union as part of a cultural exchange with the United States.

Although Louis's life was so successful, he went through some very hard times. When he left reform school, Louis wanted to be a jazz musician, but he could not even afford a cornet. He borrowed a friend's and worked at odd jobs until he could buy his own second-hand cornet. While he was still working with local New Orleans bands, Louis wrote a song, "I Wish I Could Shimmy Like My Sister Kate." A company published it but never paid him nor gave him credit as the composer.

Louis had an especially tough time in the 1930s. His manager was incompetent. Not only did he get Louis into debt, but also he arranged so many concerts that Louis had problems with his lip. It split open when he played.

Eventually, Louis fired his manager and hired Joe Glaser. Joe helped Louis get out of debt. He convinced Louis to play popular music to attract a wider audience. Many of Louis's fans criticized him for this and turned to other jazz musicians. But by the late 1940s, Louis concentrated on jazz again.

"What a Wonderful World" was a hit single in 1968.

During the last twenty years of his life, Louis was considered one of the greatest jazz singers in the world and by far the greatest trumpet player. He had long been known as Satchmo, which is a shortened version of satchel-mouth. He was given this nickname because of his large mouth—it seemed as big as a traveling bag, or satchel. Now he was hailed as Satchmo the Great. He traveled all over the world and became an "ambassador" of jazz. He continued to perform and make recordings almost to the end of his life.

Louis and his wife Lucille in June, 1970.

In March, 1971, Louis had a heart attack and was put in the hospital to recover. On July 5 of that year, he felt well enough to set up a rehearsal with his band. The next day, Louis died at home in his sleep.

Special Interests

- In the 1960s, many British colonies in Africa, such as Ghana and Nigeria, became independent countries. Louis visited these countries to give concerts and meet the people.
- Louis was fond of eating and, even when his doctors told him to, found it hard to diet. He especially loved Chinese food. Louis passed out free diet sheets to thousands of fans. He was always recommending some special diet.

Miles Davis

Family: Married first wife, Irene 1943, (divorced); married Frances Taylor, 1960s, (divorced); married third wife, 1967, (divorced); married Cicely Tyson, 1981, (divorced). Had three children, Cheryl, Gregory, and Miles IV.

Awards: New Star on Trumpet Award, *Down Beat,* 1946; New Star Award, *Esquire,* 1947; Outstanding Jazz Personality of the Year, *Down Beat*, 1958; Grammys in 1970, 1982, 1986, 1989; nominated for fourteen Grammys; *The Birth of the Cool* inducted into the National Academy of Recording Arts and Sciences (NARAS) Hall of Fame, 1982; Lifetime Achievement Award, NARAS, 1990; numerous other awards from readers' polls in *Down Beat* and other jazz magazines.

Personality Profile

Career: Trumpet player and composer.

Born: May 25, 1926, in Alton, Illinois, to Miles and Cleota Davis.

Died: September 28, 1991, in Santa Monica, California.

Education: Juilliard School of Music.

Growing Up

The son of a dentist and a violin player, Miles grew up in a comfortable home in East St. Louis, Illinois. Unlike many jazz musicians, he had an easy, secure childhood. His parents were pleased that he was interested in music, and they gave him a trumpet for his thirteenth birthday.

Miles practiced for hours each day. He was happiest when he was playing his trumpet. He played in his high school band, and in 1941, when he was fifteen, he joined a professional band, Eddie Randall's Blue Devils. While still in his teens, Miles had the chance to play with two of his jazz heroes—Dizzy Gillespie and Charlie Parker. They were visiting St. Louis, and their trumpet player became sick. Miles was thrilled when he was asked to take his place for three weeks.

While he was still in high school, Miles was making a name for himself as a jazz musician.

When Miles was eighteen, his parents enrolled him at the Juilliard School of Music in New York to study classical music. But his passion was jazz. He began to haunt the clubs where Dizzy Gillespie and others were playing. Soon he was joining them in jam sessions— informal get-togethers for music-making. Here he had the chance to play with the finest jazz musicians and to develop his own special style.

Developing Skills

"The way you change and help music is by tryin' to invent new ways to play."

Miles's trumpet playing was known for its lack of vibrato: it was smooth rather than throbbing. This was very unusual. Miles believed that good musicians had to try new ways to play. Throughout his life, Miles experimented with many different styles of music.

In 1945, at the age of nineteen, Miles made one of the first recordings of the type of music known as bebop, a fast and complex style of jazz. He made this recording with Dizzy Gillespie and other pioneers of bebop. In 1948, he formed his own nine-piece band and developed a style called cool jazz. This group made eight records that are jazz classics. In late 1955, Miles formed a quintet that included John Coltrane on tenor saxophone. This was the turning point of Miles's career. The group made five remarkable albums in 1955.

Miles played more for his own pleasure than for money. He often turned down bookings if he did not feel like playing.

The following year, Miles joined with music arranger Gil Evans to try combining jazz and orchestral music. This resulted in the album *Miles Ahead* (1957). Miles and Gil made several other successful records in this style. Meanwhile, Miles was experimenting with a style of jazz that used scales rather than chords.

In the 1960s, Miles was intrigued by the new electronics that were being used in music-making. Here was another way to make jazz sound different. By using electronics to blend together different types of music, Miles invented "fusion." His first album in this style was *Bitches Brew* (1970).

Throughout his life, Miles continued to experiment. His later recordings included rock music and pop songs. "To be a great musician you've got to be open to what's new," he said. "You have to be able to absorb it if you're going to grow and communicate your music." Miles did more than communicate. His music brought him millions of fans throughout the world.

Miles at the Newport Jazz Festival.

Accomplishments

1945	Began recording at nineteen years old.	**1957**	Released *Miles Ahead*.
1948	Formed his own group.	**1970**	Released *Bitches Brew*.
1949	Performed at the Paris Jazz Festival.	**1981**	Performed at the Kool Jazz Festival.
1955	Made five albums with John Coltrane.	**1990**	Lifetime Achievement Award, NARAS.

Overcoming Obstacles

"A guy's got to have something that challenges his imagination. That's what I tell all my musicians."

Miles suffered from diabetes and sickle-cell anemia, a hereditary blood disease. His health became even worse when he took up smoking—and worse still when he began experimenting with drugs. Miles became addicted to heroin, and in the 1950s, he was arrested. These charges were later dropped.

When Miles played, he kept his body still and the bell of his horn pointed to the floor.

In the early 1950s, it looked as if Miles's career was finished. His attempts to produce "different" music had brought him some bad reviews. His drug habit seemed to be killing him, and his private life was a mess. He had become a husband and father at the age of eighteen, but that marriage ended in divorce.

Yet just when everyone had written off Miles, he took hold of himself and made a comeback. With an incredible effort, he kicked the heroin habit. He then formed a new group, and in 1955, he was a big hit at the Newport Jazz Festival. During the 1960s and 1970s, he made many brilliant recordings which received rave reviews.

Miles had more bad luck in 1972 when he broke both his legs in a car crash. He was in poor health and for several years did not even pick up his trumpet.

Miles never took much notice of his audiences and made no effort to encourage his fans. He usually played with his back to them so that he could face the band. He seemed a strange and brooding person, which added to his attraction. He was nicknamed the Prince of Darkness. Yet it was his music, rather than his personality, that attracted most of his fans. They loved the unusual and wonderful sounds he produced with his trumpet.

Miles had one of his greatest successes in 1981 with his concerts at the Kool Jazz Festival. Leading a new group of young players, he then went on tours of North America, Europe, and Japan. Right until the end of his life, he remained a major figure in the jazz world. His death at age sixty-five shocked his fans and all the musical world.

Miles at the premiere of the movie **Jungle Fever** *in 1991.*

Special Interests

- Electric guitars and other electronics came into use during Miles's career. He was fascinated by the way this technology could be used to make music sound different.
- Miles was a good boxer and worked out regularly at gyms, even when on tour.

Duke Ellington

Personality Profile

Career: Bandleader, composer, and pianist.

Born: Edward Kennedy Ellington, April 29, 1899, in Washington, D.C., to James and Daisy Ellington.

Died: May 24, 1974, in New York City, New York.

Education: Armstrong High School, Washington, D.C.

Family: Married Edna Thompson, 1918, (separated). Had one son, Mercer.

Awards: Grammys, 1959, 1966, 1967, 1968, 1971, 1972, 1976; nominated for four more Grammys; Lifetime Achievement Award, National Academy of Recording Arts and Sciences (NARAS), 1966; Presidential Medal of Freedom, 1969; elected to the National Institute of Arts and Letters, 1970; French Legion of Honor, 1973; three records inducted into the NARAS Hall of Fame, "Mood Indigo" in 1975, "Take the 'A' Train" in 1976, and "Black, Brown, and Beige" in 1990.

Growing Up

When Edward Ellington was a teenager, he was nicknamed "Duke" by his friends because he seemed so classy and elegant. He always looked stylish. Duke grew up in a happy home. Although his parents were not wealthy, they worked hard to provide for their children's needs. For much of his boyhood, Duke lived in a pleasant neighborhood in Washington, D.C.

Both of Duke's parents were very religious, and they started him on the piano when he was six, hoping he would later play the church organ. But Duke had other ideas. He hated his piano lessons, and he disliked his teacher. He called her "Miss Clinkscales." When he was seven, she refused to teach him any more. He was the only child to forget his part in her annual music recital. Duke then taught himself, experimenting with making unusual sounds.

Duke composed his first jazz piece when he was fifteen, memorizing it on the piano. He had not yet learned to write or read music. The piece was called "Soda Fountain Rag." Duke thought it up while working at an after-school job in a soda shop.

During high school, Duke had some formal music lessons. But he quit school in his senior year. By then, he was more interested in playing jazz than in school work, and he believed he had learned enough musical theory to begin a career as a jazz musician.

"Music is my mistress, and she plays second fiddle to no one."

Duke posing for a picture in 1933.

Developing Skills

"The writing and playing of music is a matter of intent....You can't take doodling seriously."

Duke played the piano in various jazz groups until 1918, when he formed his own band. His first band was called Duke's Serenaders. He later formed several other bands, and although they had different names, they included many of the same musicians.

Duke moved to New York in 1923, and a few years later, his band began to play regularly at the popular Cotton Club in Harlem. This made him very well known because the Cotton Club performances were broadcast on the radio. People throughout the country came to know Duke's music. Its lush melodies and strange discords were very different from the usual band music. The public loved it.

Duke traveled throughout the United States during this period, and in 1933, his band made its first tour of Europe. Duke had become famous there, too, because of the many recordings of his music. Songs such as "It Don't Mean a Thing" were very popular. His band was also in great demand to play in Broadway revues and Hollywood movies. During the 1930s, Duke and his band appeared in several films, including *The Hit Parade.*

Duke was well known as both a performer and a composer.

Duke wrote more than two thousand pieces of music during his career. Many were popular songs such as "In a Sentimental Mood." Others were jazz symphonies. One of the best known of these is *Black, Brown, and Beige* which he first performed in 1943. It is about the history and music of African Americans.

In 1947, the government of Liberia, a country in Africa, asked Duke to write *Liberian Suite* to celebrate the country's hundredth birthday. He had another great honor when the famous Italian conductor Arturo Toscanini paid him to write *Harlem* for the NBC Symphony Orchestra in 1950. In 1969, on Duke's seventieth birthday, he received one of his greatest honors. At a party at the White House, President Richard Nixon awarded him the Presidential Medal of Freedom, the highest civilian honor in the United States.

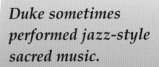

Duke sometimes performed jazz-style sacred music.

Accomplishments

1918 Formed Duke's Serenaders.

1927-32 Performed at the Cotton Club.

1933 First tour of Europe.

1943 Performed *Black, Brown, and Beige* at Carnegie Hall.

1956 Performed at the Newport Jazz Festival.

1965 Performed at the White House Festival of the Arts.

1966 Lifetime Achievement Award, NARAS.

1969 Awarded Presidential Medal of Freedom.

Overcoming Obstacles

Duke was lucky to be raised in a loving home, but he still faced several problems. His first obstacle was his parents' plans for his musical career. But Duke was determined to become a jazz musician rather than a church organist.

Duke was known as a calm and generous man to his fellow musicians and fans.

When Duke first started playing in jazz clubs at the age of eighteen, he could not earn enough to support himself. Since he had a talent for painting as well as music, he took a daytime job painting commercial signs. It was not the job he wanted, but it allowed him to pursue his jazz career in the evenings. Jazz was everything to Duke. It totally absorbed him. "I just don't have time to be a social cat," he once said.

Although Duke did not have much formal training on the piano, he refused to enter a music school as some people advised. Many people believe his lack of training allowed him to create the new sounds for which he was well known.

When the rhythmic "swing" jazz that he played went out of fashion in the 1940s, Duke became very depressed. Bebop, a fast-paced style of jazz, was all the rage. The era of the big bands seemed to be over.

In 1949, *Down Beat* magazine said it was time for Duke to disband his orchestra. The public felt the same. Duke had a difficult time until 1956, when he made a comeback at the Newport Jazz Festival. Suddenly, Duke and his orchestra were popular again.

A 1965 Pulitzer Prize music jury recommended that Duke be given a special prize for his achievements. When the Pulitzer board ignored the recommendation, Duke simply responded that "fate doesn't want me to be famous too young."

Throughout his career, Duke gained millions of fans all over the world. His overseas tours in the 1960s and early 1970s took him as far away as India, South America, and Australia. By then, he was being called the greatest jazz composer ever.

Throughout his life, Duke continued to paint as a hobby.

Special Interests

- Duke was a talented painter. He was especially good at watercolors.
- From 1943 to 1955, Duke helped set up and organize the jazz concerts given at Carnegie Hall each year.
- Duke was very concerned about his health. He tried to sleep nine or ten hours a day, and he took a lot of vitamins.

Billie Holiday

Personality Profile

Career: Singer.

Born: Eleanora Fagan, April 7, 1915, in Baltimore, Maryland, to Sadie Fagan and Clarence Holiday.

Died: July 17, 1959, in New York City, New York.

Family: Married James Monroe, 1941, (divorced, 1956); married Louis McKay, 1956, (separated).

Awards: *Esquire* gold award, 1944 and 1947; *Esquire* silver award, 1945 and 1946; winner of *Metronome* poll as Best Female Singer, 1945-46; Grammy nominations, 1961, 1973; Lifetime Achievement Award, National Academy of Recording Arts and Sciences (NARAS), 1987; two albums inducted into the NARAS Hall of Fame, *Strange Fruit* in 1978, and *Lover Man (Oh, Where Can You Be?)* in 1989.

Growing Up

When Billie was born, she was named Eleanora Fagan, taking her unmarried mother's surname. Her parents were teenagers, and they were still teenagers when they married three years later. Soon after that, the marriage broke up. Billie seldom saw her father, a jazz musician who traveled around the country.

Billie's mother could not support her family on her small salary as a domestic worker, so she left Billie with her relatives. They lived in a rough section of town and in crowded conditions. However, Billie loved being with her great-grandmother who had been a slave on a plantation.

When Billie was ten, she was raped by a neighbor and then blamed for the attack. She was sent to a reform school and told she must stay there until she was twenty-one. Two years later, as punishment for some small action, she was locked in a room with a dead body. When her mother heard of this, she managed to get Billie released from the reformatory.

"If you find a tune that's got something to do with you, you just feel it; and when you sing it, other people feel it too."

Billie then went to live with her mother who had rented some cheap rooms in a Harlem brothel. Since they needed money to live, Billie became a prostitute. Before long, she was arrested. She dreaded going back to the reformatory, so she and her mother told the judge she was eighteen. Thirteen-year-old Billie spent the next four months in an adult prison.

Developing Skills

As a young child, Billie had often listened to records of the famous blues singer Bessie Smith, and she longed to be a singer too. When Billie was fifteen, her mother got sick and could not work. Billie tried to get hired as a singer or dancer in the local night spots in Harlem. At first, she had no luck. Finally, the owner of a basement bar agreed to give her a try.

Although Billie had no training as a singer, the customers liked her, and she was hired on the spot. She was soon performing in several Harlem clubs. Her big break came in 1932 when she was discovered by John Hammond, a record producer. She made her first recording the following year with Benny Goodman's orchestra. Gradually, more people learned about Billie's talent, and in 1935, she was booked for a week at the Apollo Theater in Harlem. This was her big break. Billie's performance brought her wide attention and rave reviews.

Billie performed with Lionel Hampton at the Metropolitan Opera House in 1944.

Billie had a unique way of singing, a slow and lazy drawl that was different from the usual blues style. At other times, her songs were light and bouncy. Whichever style she chose, she added something special to the music. Her singing touched people's emotions. Her appearance was striking as well. She usually wore gardenias in her hair. With her eyes half closed, she swayed as she sang. A fellow musician was so impressed that he gave her the nickname "Lady Day." The name stuck.

Lady Day was at the peak of her career in the late 1930s. She sang in popular New York clubs and toured with Count Basie's orchestra. In l938, she was hired as the female soloist in Artie Shaw's white band.

Billie's health suffered from years of drug and alcohol abuse. In her recordings of the 1950s, even her voice began to weaken. She still moved her listeners, however, with the emotions she put into her songs.

Billy usually wore gardenias in her hair when she performed.

Accomplishments

1930 Began career in Harlem clubs.

1933 Made first record with the Benny Goodman Orchestra.

1937 Toured with Count Basie's Orchestra.

1938 Joined Artie Shaw's band.

1946 Appeared in the movie *New Orleans*.

1956 Published her life story, *Lady Sings the Blues*.

1972 Diana Ross stars in a film based on Billie's life, *Lady Sings the Blues*.

1987 Lifetime Achievement Award, NARAS.

Overcoming Obstacles

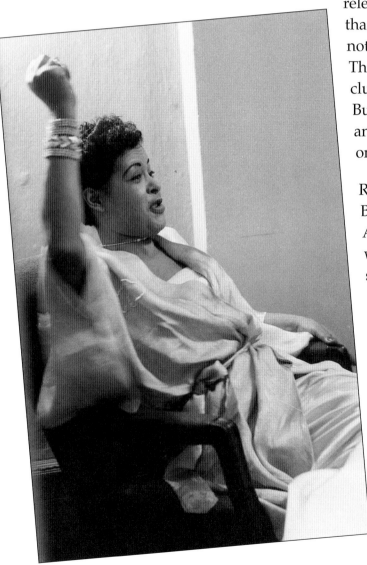

"I hate straight singing. What comes out is what I feel."

Billie's life was full of professional success as well as personal tragedy. She was only forty-four when she died. Billie did most of her work in clubs and bars, and she began abusing alcohol at an early age. Worse still, her first husband introduced her to heroin and opium. Billie struggled against drug addiction for many years. In the 1940s, she was sent to prison on drug charges. When she was released, she was banned from places that sold liquor. This meant she could not sing in the New York nightclubs. The ban was a bitter blow because the clubs provided her main audience. But she still performed in theaters and made recordings. She also went on tour to Europe.

Racism was another problem Billie faced throughout her life. As an African-American singer with Artie Shaw's white band, she had a difficult time, even though the band tried to protect her. Things were particularly hard when they were on tour. Restaurants would not let Billie eat with her fellow musicians. She could not stay in the same hotels. When she tried to do so, she was told there was no room. She was not even allowed to enter theaters by the main door but had to use the back door. This made her furious.

Billie poured out her anger into her music. One of her most successful songs was about racism. It was called "Strange Fruit." The strange fruit are black men who have been lynched and are hanging from the trees. The song was so powerful that some places banned it. Yet it was a major hit. It remains one of Billie's most moving songs.

Despite her difficult life, Billie rose to the top of her profession and made a unique contribution to jazz. She is considered one of the world's greatest jazz singers. Today, millions of people still enjoy listening to her recordings.

Billie performing around 1939.

Special Interests

- Billie loved dogs and always had one with her. She felt she could trust dogs more than people.
- Billie enjoyed knitting and crocheting. She knitted to pass the time when on tour.

Thelonious Monk

Personality Profile

Career: Pianist and composer.

Born: October 10, 1917, in Rocky Mount, North Carolina, to Thelonious and Barbara Monk.

Died: February 17, 1982, in Englewood, New Jersey.

Family: Married Nellie Smith. Had two children, Thelonious, Jr., and Barbara.

Awards: Top of *Down Beat* magazine's critics' poll, 1958, 1959; Intercities Award for Most Outstanding Jazz Pianist, 1958, 1959, and 1969; nominated for Grammy, 1963; honored with a special tribute at President Jimmy Carter's White House jazz party, 1978; Grammy for Best Historical Album, 1987.

Growing Up

When Thelonious was barely two years old, he was already picking out tunes on the piano. By the time he was five, he had learned to read music by watching his sister's piano lessons. He showed so much talent that his mother saved up to buy him a baby grand piano. It almost filled their two-room apartment in Harlem.

Thelonious's family had moved from North Carolina to Harlem when he was four. His father soon returned to the South, leaving his family very short of money. Even so, his mother made sure that Thelonious took lessons from a skilled piano teacher. She understood Thelonious's love of music. She herself was very musical and sang in the choir at the local Baptist church.

For two years, Thelonious played the piano and organ at the Baptist church, but it was jazz that he loved. By the time he was thirteen, he was performing at local events and in neighborhood bars. Already he was a polished player. He played so well that he regularly won the talent contests at Harlem's Apollo Theater. Finally, the manager had to ban him from taking part so that others could have a chance to win.

"When I was a kid, if anybody sat down and played the piano, I would just stand there and watch 'em all the time."

Developing Skills

Thelonious left high school when he was sixteen. He spent the next two years on tour, playing the piano for a faith healer and preacher. He then returned to New York where he worked as a pianist in a number of Harlem clubs.

Thelonious was as well known for his goatee and strange hats as he was for his unusual performing style.

In the early 1940s, Thelonious was hired by Minton's Playhouse, one of the most famous Harlem clubs. Trumpeter Dizzy Gillespie and saxophonist Charlie Parker also played there. The musicians often stayed on after the club closed, trying out new ideas and techniques. Thelonious stayed on with them, letting his imagination run free. Together they created a new style of jazz. Thelonious first called it bipbop, but was misunderstood. Bebop was born.

Thelonious was always experimenting, trying new ways of making jazz sound different. Around 1951, he composed some of his best pieces, including "Blue Monk" and "Round Midnight." Although it took years for his piano playing to be appreciated, his compositions were recognized early in his career. In 1954, he released his first solo album, *Pure Monk*, and that same year he gave his first overseas concerts on a visit to France.

By 1960, Thelonious had hundreds of thousands of fans. They loved his odd behavior almost as much as they loved his music. In the middle of playing, he might stand up and wander around or do a little dance. Sometimes he played the piano with his elbows as well as his fingers. He and his fellow musicians used phrases such as "groovy" and "cool, baby."

As his fame grew, Thelonious performed at some of the nation's major concert halls, including Lincoln Center and Carnegie Hall, both in New York City. In the early 1960s, he toured in Japan and Europe, and in 1964, he was featured on the cover of *Time* magazine. After more successful overseas touring in the the early 1970s, Thelonious gave a memorable final concert in Carnegie Hall in 1976.

It took many years for people to recognize Thelonious's great talent.

Accomplishments

Early 1940s House pianist at Minton's Playhouse.

1954 Released first solo album, *Pure Monk.*

1959 Formed his own big band.

1962 Offered a recording contract by Columbia Records.

1964 Featured on the cover of *Time* magazine.

1976 Last concert at Carnegie Hall.

1989 Documentary about his life, *Straight, No Chaser.*

Overcoming Obstacles

"As for the hard times I've had, I've never been jealous of any musician.... I kept on making it— recording and doing what I'm doing, and thinking. While they were talking, I was thinking music and still trying to play."

Despite his talent, Thelonious had great difficulty finding work during the 1940s and early 1950s. Having drifted away from mainstream jazz, he was on the fringes of the jazz world. Year after year, he struggled to make a living, playing in dance halls and bars, usually for very low wages. Sometimes he earned as little as twenty dollars a week.

In 1951, Thelonious and a friend were arrested when the police found some heroin in their car. Thelonious was not a heroin addict, but out of loyalty to his friend, he shared the blame for the drugs. He was jailed for two months. Worse still, he was banned from playing in places that sold liquor. Since most of the clubs and dance halls sold liquor, the ban pretty well put Thelonious out of work.

Rather than giving in to despair, Thelonious decided to concentrate on writing and recording music. Meanwhile, his wife worked as a clerk to support the family. Thelonious had other help too. He had attracted the attention of a rich jazz fan, the Baroness de Koenigswarter, who helped the family with money from time to time. Often, she invited Thelonious and his family to stay in her apartment. He composed some of his best music there.

When the ban on playing in clubs was lifted, Thelonious made a successful comeback, leading his own quartet at the Five Spot Café in New York City's Greenwich Village. Even when he was arrested for rowdiness in 1958 and banned for another two years, his career continued. Finally, after years of struggle, Thelonious's work received widespread recognition in the 1950s. Many now praised his contributions to jazz music. Musicians such as John Coltrane and Sonny Rollins named Thelonious as the most important influence on their work.

Thelonious continued to record, toured widely, and formed a ten-piece band. Until his health began to fail in the mid-1970s, he was one of the most sought-after jazz musicians in the world. He retired from touring and recording in the 1970s.

Thelonious and his quartet at the New York Jazz Festival in 1975.

Special Interests

- Thelonious liked to wear unusual hats. He might appear on stage wearing a big Chinese straw hat, an embroidered skullcap from Africa, or a fur cap. Nobody ever knew what to expect.

Charlie Parker

Personality Profile

Career: Saxophone player and composer.

Born: August 29, 1920, in Kansas City, Missouri, to Charles and Addie Parker.

Died: March 12, 1955, in New York City, New York.

Education: Lincoln High School.

Family: Married Rebecca Ruffin, 1936, (divorced); married Geraldine Scott, 1943, (divorced); married Doris Snyder, 1948, (divorced); married Chan Richardson, 1950. Had two sons, Francis and Baird; a daughter, Pree; and an adopted daughter, Kim.

Awards: New Star Award, 1946; elected to the *Down Beat* Hall of Fame, 1955; Grammy for Best Jazz Performance by a Soloist, 1974; Lifetime Achievement Award, National Academy of Recording Arts and Sciences (NARAS), 1984; two albums inducted into the NARAS Hall of Fame, *Charlie Parker with Strings* in 1988, and *Ornithology* in 1989.

Growing Up

Charlie was known to his fellow musicians as Yardbird, or Bird. He was born and raised in Kansas City—first in Kansas City, Kansas, and then across the river in Kansas City, Missouri, not far from the theater district. This was a lively part of town, full of dance halls and nightclubs where jazz was played well into the night. Charlie found it very exciting and was eager to make music himself. In high school, he learned to play the horn and the saxophone, and in 1934, when he was fourteen, he dropped out of school to become a musician.

At this time, Charlie was still very much a beginner and did not play well. But he was eager to learn. Realizing this, the local musicians let him join in their jam sessions—informal get-togethers for music-making. At one of these sessions, Charlie made so many mistakes that the drummer lost his temper and threw his cymbals at Charlie's feet.

"Music is your own experience. If you don't live it, it won't come out of your horn."

This incident was very upsetting, but it did not stop Charlie. Determined to play better, he began to listen carefully to the best players, noting their techniques. Gradually, his playing improved. By the time he was sixteen, he played well enough to get a job with a small band.

> *"They say music speaks louder than words, so we'd rather voice our opinion that way."*

Charlie performed with several groups during the next few years, traveling to the Ozarks, Chicago, and New York. He played both alto and tenor saxophone, but he preferred the alto sax. As he gained confidence, he developed a bold and fiery style. It amazed and delighted the musicians who heard him. They joked that his playing was so powerful it could blow them out of the room.

In the late 1930s, Charlie performed as a soloist with Jay McShann's group, and during the next few years, he made some memorable recordings. These included his hit "Confessin' the Blues." Around this time, Charlie first met the trumpeter Dizzy Gillespie. The two men became good friends and were impressed by each other's playing.

Charlie with Dizzy Gillespie in 1950.

During the next few years, Charlie and Dizzy performed together with several well-known groups, including Billy Eckstine's band. They also played together after their performances were over. At these jam sessions, they had no audience to please, so they could play how they liked. They experimented with new sounds and new types of rhythm, responding to each other's ideas. They developed the fast-paced style of jazz that came to be called bebop.

The pianist Thelonious Monk also took part in these jam sessions. Dizzy credits the creation of bebop to Charlie, insisting that Charlie was "the architect" of the new sound. "He knew how to get from one note to another, the style of the thing," said Dizzy. "Most of what I did was in the area of harmony and rhythm."

In 1947, Charlie formed his own quintet which toured the United States and Europe. It was a great hit at the Paris Jazz Festival in 1949. That same year, Charlie recorded "Bird with Strings" which became his biggest seller. By this time, he had a great reputation, especially among jazz musicians. They listened to his music with awe and tried to copy his style. A club called Birdland was named in his honor.

Charlie performing at Birdland after its opening in 1949.

Accomplishments

1938 Joined Jay McShann's group.

1942-43 Played with Earl Hines's band.

1944-46 Played with Billy Eckstine's band.

1947 Formed his own quintet.

1949 Performed at Paris Jazz Festival.

1984 Lifetime Achievement Award, NARAS.

1988 The movie *Bird* about Charlie Parker's life, was screened at the Cannes Film Festival. The film was directed by Clint Eastwood.

Overcoming Obstacles

Charlie began to abuse drugs and alcohol when he was a teenager, and he struggled with the problem all his life. Despite his talent, he was often fired because of his drug use. He seldom stayed with any band for long. He even missed performances. Charlie moved to Chicago and then to New York to find work. For a while, he washed dishes at Jimmy's Chicken Shack to support himself.

He continued to work with jazz greats such as Sarah Vaughan, but he lost jobs because of his drug habit. Even musicians who admired Charlie's talent had little patience for his lifestyle. Charlie later said that his problems with drugs came from "being introduced too early to nightclub life."

On the West Coast in 1946, Charlie went through a particularly bad period. He collapsed after a recording session and had a nervous breakdown. He spent the next six months in the hospital, trying to overcome his heroin addiction. For a while, he succeeded. The next few years were probably his best. After he came out of hospital, he played better than ever, and he gained thousands of new fans during a successful tour of Europe.

Charlie with Swedish drummer Sven Bollhem and Max Roach in 1949.

Sadly, Charlie then went downhill again. Hoping to lessen his craving for heroin, he began to drink heavily. His drinking affected his music and made him so difficult that people would not work with him. In his depressed state, Charlie tried to kill himself in 1954. Once again, he ended up in the hospital. He recovered and gave a brilliant performance a few months later, but he had misused his body for too long. He died the following year, at the age of thirty-four.

Even though Charlie died young, he had a major effect on jazz. Few musicians have left such a mark. He is still remembered as one of the greatest of the jazz "greats." The famous trumpet player Cootie Williams considered Charlie the greatest. Explaining why, Cootie said, "Every instrument in the band tried to copy Charlie Parker, and in the history of jazz there had never been one man who influenced all the instruments."

Charlie performing with the Birdland Band.

Special Interests

- Charlie thought it important to encourage young musicians. He took time to help them perfect their style, giving them hints on how to play better.
- Charlie liked to listen to classical music. He especially admired the work of modern composers such as Delius and Prokofiev.

Bessie Smith

Personality Profile

Career: Singer.

Born: April 15, 1895, in Chattanooga, Tennessee, to William and Laura Smith.

Died: September 26, 1937, in Clarksdale, Mississippi.

Family: Married Earl Love, 1918, (died); married Jack Gee, 1923. Had one adopted son, Jack Gee, Jr.

Awards: *Empty Bed Blues* inducted into the National Academy of Recording Arts and Science (NARAS) Hall of Fame, 1983; inducted into the National Women's Hall of Fame, 1984; Lifetime Achievement Award, NARAS, 1989.

Growing Up

Bessie performing in 1925.

"**A** little ramshackle cabin" was how Bessie described the shack where she was born and raised. Like most other African Americans in Chattanooga, Tennessee, her parents had little money. They could barely afford to feed their children, let alone hire a doctor. Two of Bessie's brothers died young, and by the time she was nine, both her parents had also died.

Bessie's oldest sister, Viola, took in washing to support the family. There were six of them—four girls and two boys. Sometimes the children earned a few cents by performing in the streets. Bessie would sing while her brother Andrew played the guitar.

When Bessie was fourteen, she joined a variety troupe that was visiting Chattanooga. During the next few years, she toured with several such groups. They moved from town to town, setting up a tent in each place and charging a small admission fee. Bessie started out as a dancer in the chorus, but after a few years, she was doing a solo act. The audiences loved her rich, deep singing voice. In the days before microphones, Bessie's voice could fill a hall.

"Bessie Smith was the greatest artist American jazz ever produced; in fact, I'm not sure that her art did not reach beyond the limits of the term 'jazz.' ...She was...capable of projecting her whole personality into music."
– John Hammond, 1937

Developing Skills

"More than any other singer, she set the blues tradition."

I n 1912, Bessie joined a group that included Ma Rainie, "the Mother of the Blues." This was a big break. By watching Ma and listening to her singing, Bessie learned a lot about her own craft. Within a few years, she was putting on her own shows and performing in theaters as well as tents. She did so well that she was able to buy a house in Philadelphia.

It was not just Bessie's strong and deep voice that made her popular. It was the way she sang and the things she sang about that appealed to her fans. At a time when pop songs were about imaginary romances, Bessie sang of real-life problems, such as losing a boyfriend, being hungry, or not having a job. Often she added a touch of comedy or put on a sad smile, as if saying to her listeners, "I know you'll understand." Many in her audience did indeed understand.

Bessie's first record in 1923 was an instant success. It sold 780,000 copies in the first six months. It was produced by Columbia Records, a company that was not doing well at the time. Once Bessie signed on, Columbia's fortunes improved. During the next ten years, she made 160 records with Columbia. On some recordings she was accompanied by such famous jazz musicians as trumpeter Louis Armstrong. "St. Louis Blues" and "Nashville Woman's Blues" were two famous songs she recorded with Louis.

Bessie's records brought her a large audience. She now had fans across the country. They called her the Empress of the Blues. Her shows were sell-outs, and long lines of adoring fans wanted to see her.

Until the day she died, Bessie continued to give concerts and make records. She switched her singing style to the fast-paced "swing" that was becoming popular. Yet it is for her blues music that Bessie is best remembered. One of the greatest blues singers of all time, she inspired Billie Holiday and many other younger artists. Today, she is still known as one of the most important singers in the history of jazz.

Bessie in 1923 in one of her concert costumes.

Accomplishments

1912 Joined Ma Rainie's group.	**1933** Last recording session.
1923 Recorded the songs "Down-Hearted Blues" and "Gulf Coast Blues."	**1936** Appeared in a revue at the Apollo Theater, Harlem.
1929 Starred in the movie *St. Louis Blues*.	**1989** Lifetime Achievement Award, NARAS.

Overcoming Obstacles

At the height of Bessie's popularity, when she was a top-ranking star, the main thing that many white Americans noticed about her was the color of her skin. Because she was black, restaurant owners turned her away. Hotels would not admit her. Touring was a miserable business because she had to face such racism every day.

By 1924, Bessie had sold over 2 million records.

To make things more pleasant for herself and her troupe, Bessie bought a large railroad car in 1925. She had it painted and decorated and fitted it with furniture. For a while, they all traveled in comfort. But when work became scarce during the Depression, Bessie could not afford to keep the rail car.

Bessie also had a difficult marriage with Jack Gee. They fought and broke up many times. After one break up in 1929, Jack Gee kept their adopted son from Bessie for years, moving from boarding house to boarding house so that she could not find them.

Bessie had several very difficult years in the early 1930s. People had so little money to spend that they listened to the radio instead of going to the theater. People could not afford to buy records. Many theaters had to close and record companies had to cut back. Meanwhile, blues music was beginning to sound old-fashioned. To survive as a singer, Bessie changed her style. She began to sing in the swing style and was once again in demand as a performer.

Several years earlier, Bessie had performed in the film *St. Louis Blues*, and now there was talk of another film. But just as things seemed to be getting better, Bessie was badly hurt in a car crash. On September 25, 1937, she was traveling overnight from Tennessee to Mississippi for her next show. Just north of Clarksdale, Mississippi, her car hit a parked truck. Although a surgeon who was passing by the accident tried to save her, Bessie died in the hospital a few hours later.

Bessie was known as the Empress of the Blues because of her talent.

Special Interests

- Bessie was brought up a Baptist and was very religious. Some of her blues songs sound almost like hymns.
- Bessie loved to garden and fulfilled her wish when she bought a farmhouse in New Jersey.

Cindy Blackman

Cindy had been fascinated by the drums since she was a small child.

W hen Cindy was sixteen, she heard the drummer Tony Williams play in her local music store. That is what drumming ought to be, she thought. It should be a major part of the band, not just a background to other music.

Cindy had been fascinated by the drums since she was a small child. For years, she had begged her parents for a drum set, and eventually they bought her one. She played the drums every day. She played before school, after school—every moment she could get. She studied hard to improve her technique. After school, she took lessons in classical percussion at the University of Hartford in Hartford, Connecticut.

Cindy's family was very musical. Almost everyone played the piano, and most could play other instruments as well. Both Cindy's mother and grandmother were classical musicians, and Cindy was expected to follow in their footsteps. But it was jazz Cindy loved, not the classics. Although she went on to study at Boston's Berklee College of Music, she stayed only three semesters. New York City was where the action was, and that was where Cindy headed.

Cindy arrived in New York in 1982 and played wherever she could—in clubs, in a few concerts, even on the sidewalk. Her drumming quickly attracted notice. She played with tremendous energy and style, putting her whole body into it. She has said that the drums "can really shake things up," and she certainly shook up her listeners. She made such an impression that in 1984 she was featured on New York radio in the program "Jazz Stars of the Future."

Personality Profile

Career: Drummer and composer.

Born: November 18, 1959, in Yellow Springs, Ohio.

Education: West Hartford High School; University of Hartford; Berklee College of Music.

Meanwhile, Cindy was also composing. Two of her pieces appeared on an album in 1987. When an executive at Muse Records heard them, he immediately offered Cindy a recording contract. She would lead her own band, he said, and play her own music. The first record on which she appeared as composer, bandleader, and drummer was *Arcane*, which was released in 1988. Four years later, she brought out her second album, *Code Red*.

During these years, Cindy played and recorded with other groups as well as her own. She also went on overseas tours. In 1993, she teamed up with rock singer Lenny Kravitz. Lenny heard Cindy play over the phone and immediately flew her out to audition for him. He signed her on with his band. Rock was a big change from the more freestyle type of jazz she had been playing. A further change came with her 1994 album, *Telepathy*, which many people consider her finest. She played with a quartet because she wanted the sound of a small group.

Always ready to try something new, Cindy continues to delight her listeners. "Drummers should have a lot of impact and great sound," she says. "The drums should speak just as freely as anybody." Sometimes she makes the drums "speak" in a romantic and moody voice. At other times, they are bold and dominant. Always her performance is exciting. Cindy's inventive playing has brought her many fans, both at home and overseas.

Accomplishments

1982	Began playing in New York jazz clubs.	**1993**	Began playing with Lenny Kravitz.
1987	Signed on with Muse Records.	**1994**	Released *Telepathy*.
1988	Released *Arcane*.	**1995**	Summer tour with Lenny Kravitz.
1992	Released *Code Red* and *Trio + Two*.		

Dizzy Gillespie

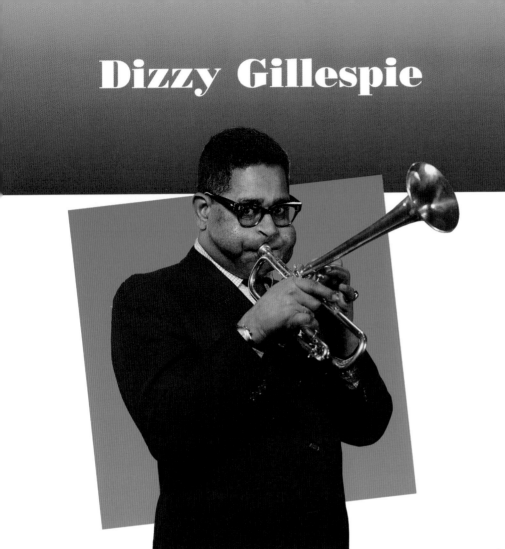

Dizzy's real name was John Birks Gillespie. He got his nickname "Dizzy" because of the way he clowned on stage. For example, having told his audience that he was going to introduce the band, he would introduce the members of the band to each other: "John, meet Max. Max, meet Ray...." His jokes always brought a laugh.

Dizzy was raised in Cheraw, South Carolina, the youngest of nine children. His father, a bricklayer, was a part-time musician. At school, Dizzy learned the trumpet and joined the school band. He played so well that he won a scholarship to the Laurinburg Technical Institute in North Carolina.

Dizzy got his nickname because of the way he clowned on stage.

Dizzy's family moved to Philadelphia when he was seventeen, and he soon began to play in the local bands. Two years later, when he went to New York City, he was already an outstanding trumpet player. At first, Dizzy did not have a job in New York, but he joined in all-night jam sessions—informal get-togethers for playing music—and became well known in jazz circles. He was hired by the Teddy Hill Orchestra to go on a European tour when he was only nineteen.

Personality Profile

Career: Trumpet player and bandleader.

Born: John Birks Gillespie, October 21, 1917, in Cheraw, South Carolina, to James and Lottie Gillespie.

Died: January 6, 1993, in Englewood, New Jersey.

Education: Laurinburg Technical Institute.

Awards: New Star Award, *Esquire*, 1944; Grammy for Best Solo Jazz Performance, 1975; Lifetime Achievement Award, National Academy of Recording Arts and Sciences (NARAS), 1989; National Medal of Arts, 1989; Duke Award, 1989; Paul Robeson Award, State of New Jersey, 1989; made a tribal chief of Nigeria, 1989; Grammy for Best Large Jazz Ensemble Performance, 1991.

Over the next few years, Dizzy played in several other famous bands. He also composed songs. One of his most famous early songs was "A Night in Tunisia." Meanwhile, with saxophonist Charlie Parker, he was developing an entirely new type of jazz. In their evening jam sessions, when they were just having fun playing music, they created the fast-paced jazz called bebop. "I guess Charlie and I had a meeting of the minds," Dizzy once said. "Both of us inspired each other."

Bebop was wildly popular in the 1940s and early 1950s. Dizzy formed his own quintet in 1944, and the following year, he formed his first big band. In 1947, his band gave a bebop concert at Carnegie Hall. Meanwhile, he was developing yet another type of music—Afro-Cuban jazz. This was a blending of Latin-American music and jazz.

In 1956, the U.S. State Department sent Dizzy on a musical tour of Africa, Asia, and the Middle East. This tour was one of many that brought him fame throughout the world. During the following years, he appeared regularly at jazz festivals all over the world, including the Newport Jazz Festival. A festival seemed to lack something if Dizzy was not there with his bulging cheeks and strange-shaped trumpet. Years earlier, someone had sat on his trumpet at a party, bending the bell upward. He liked the softer sound the bent trumpet made and continued to play it.

Dizzy did not slow down as he grew older. Although he had made his name as a master of bebop, he moved with the times, adapting to each new style of jazz. In 1989, at the age of seventy-two, he gave three hundred concerts in twenty-seven countries. He also recorded four albums, appeared on three television shows, and performed with two symphony orchestras.

Accomplishments

1937 Arrived in New York City.

1940s Developed bebop with Charlie Parker and others.

1944 Formed quintet.

1945 Formed first big band.

1947 Gave bebop concert at Carnegie Hall.

1956 Toured Africa, Asia, and the Middle East on behalf of U.S. State Department.

1967 Performed at Latin-American jazz festival in Mexico.

1977 Tour to Cuba.

1989 Lifetime Achievement Award, NARAS.

1990 Performed in Jazz Festival concert at Carnegie Hall.

Abbey Lincoln

Abbey modeled her singing after Billie Holiday and other African-American singers whose records she had heard.

T he tenth of twelve children, Abbey often felt ignored when she was young. To get attention, she took up singing. She sang as a soloist in her school and church choirs, and at nineteen, she won an amateur singing contest.

Abbey modeled her singing after Billie Holiday and other African-American singers whose records she had heard. She was determined to have a career as a performer. But there was not much chance locally. Although Abbey had been born in Chicago, her mother had moved the family to the country in Michigan, thinking it more suitable for children.

Abbey was just twenty when she first performed professionally in Jackson, Michigan. She sang under her real name, Anna Marie Wooldridge. She kept the name when she moved to California the following year, and then changed her professional name several times.

Finally, in 1956, she settled on the name Abbey Lincoln. The name was a combination of Westminster Abbey, the famous church in London, England, and Abraham Lincoln. During those years, her image was very different from her reputation today as a serious performer. "All I wanted was to be thought of as beautiful and desirable," she has said. She added to this glamorous image when she played a small part in the film *The Girl Can't Help It*. She wore the famous dress that Marilyn Monroe had worn in the movie *Gentlemen Prefer Blondes*. This dress and her performance brought her a lot of attention.

Soon, Abbey wanted to change her name. She longed to be taken seriously. She is said to have burned the Monroe dress a few years later. This was the result of meeting the great jazz drummer Max Roach, whom she later married. Rather than copying white film stars, Abbey now became a proud African American.

During the late 1950s, she became active in the civil rights movement. She sang on Max's 1960 civil rights record, *We Insist!: Freedom Now Suite*, and she spoke out boldly about the problems of African Americans. During the next few years, as Abbey performed and recorded with Max, she became a role model for many other African-American women.

Personality Profile

Career: Singer, composer, and actor.

Born: Anna Marie Wooldridge, August 6, 1930, in Chicago, Illinois.

Education: Central High School, Kalamazoo, Michigan.

Awards: Best Actress Award from the Federation of Italian Filmmakers, 1965; Best Actress Award at First World Festival of Negro Arts, 1966; Most Prominent Screen Person Award from All American Press Association, 1969; inducted into the Black Filmmakers Hall of Fame, 1975.

Abbey turned to acting in the mid-1960s and appeared in several films including *The Love of Ivy* (1968). But her marriage to Max was falling apart, and with it her career. For a while, she lived with her mother in California, where she painted and wrote poetry and music. This was a tough time for Abbey, although she had some successful trips abroad. On a visit to Africa, she was given the name Aminata by the president of Guinea, and she was named Moseka, which means goddess of love, in Zaire.

Many people thought Abbey's career was over, but in 1979, she made a comeback with her album *People in Me*. It was a stunning success. Since then, she has released a new album every few years. She has also returned to acting, both on stage and in film. She appeared in *Mo' Better Blues* in 1990.

Accomplishments

1950 First appearance as nightclub singer.

1956 First album, *A Story of a Girl in Love.*

1960 Performed on Max Roach album, *We Insist!: Freedom Now Suite.*

1968 Appeared in the movie *The Love of Ivy.*

1975 Wrote, directed, and produced the play *A Pig in a Poke.*

1979 Released the album *People in Me.*

1994 Released the album *When There Is Love* with Hank Jones.

Wynton Marsalis

Both Wynton's parents were musicians who encouraged their children's musical talents.

Wynton was raised in Kenner, near New Orleans, Louisiana, the city where jazz was invented. Both his parents were musicians who encouraged their children's musical talents. Wynton's elder brother Branford could play both the clarinet and the piano by the time he was seven. Hoping that Wynton would show the same abilities, his parents gave him a trumpet when he was six. It was not just any trumpet. It had belonged to the famous trumpeter Al Hirt, in whose band Wynton's father played.

The following year, in 1968, Wynton gave his first public performance, playing "The Marine Hymn" at a concert given by the Xavier Junior School of Music. However, he was not all that interested in music at the time. He preferred to play basketball with his friends. Basketball is still Wynton's favorite sport, but his entire life is now centered on music.

The change came when Wynton was twelve and heard a record of the famous trumpeter Clifford Brown. Until then, Wynton had not realized how wonderful the trumpet could sound. Once Wynton decided to be a trumpeter, he practiced furiously. His hard work paid off quickly. At fourteen, he won a state music competition. As a result, he was asked to play at a concert given by the New Orleans Philharmonic Orchestra. Wynton's playing was so outstanding that he was in great demand to perform locally. While still at high school, he played with several New Orleans orchestras and bands, including his brother Branford's rock group.

Wynton seemed equally brilliant no matter what type of music he played. While studying at the Juilliard School of Music in New York City in his late teens, he spent his summer vacation playing with the famous Jazz Messengers. By the time he was twenty, he had a contract with Columbia Records to record both jazz and classical music.

From then on, it was one success after the next. His first record in 1982 was nominated for a Grammy award, although it failed to win one. The following year, he won two Grammy awards, one for a classical album, the other for jazz. This achievement stunned the music world; Wynton was only twenty-two years old. He is the youngest person ever to win a Grammy award in jazz three years running.

Personality Profile

Career: Trumpet player.

Born: October 18, 1961, in New Orleans, Louisiana, to Ellis and Dolores Marsalis.

Education: New Orleans Center for Performing Arts, 1976; Berkshire Music Center's summer program, 1979; Juilliard School of Music, 1979-81.

Awards: Grammy awards as Jazz Soloist, 1983, 1984, 1985; as Classical Soloist, 1983, 1984; as Jazz Player with Group, 1985, 1986, 1987; awarded Grand Prix du Disque of France, Edison Award of the Netherlands; honorary degrees from the Manhattan College of Music, Yale University, Princeton University, and Hunter College, 1995.

Wynton's concert performances were as successful as his records. He has toured the world and is Japan's most popular jazz star. Wynton feels it is important to spread the knowledge of jazz as widely as possible. He says it is not just another type of music. It is a major form of American culture that has been given to the world. He has shocked some people by saying that he believes jazz music is more difficult to master than classical music.

In 1987, Wynton helped launch a three-year jazz education program in the Chicago school system. He often visits schools and is always eager to teach people about jazz. He keeps in touch with many of the students he meets during his visits. His many activities include being artistic director of the Classical Jazz Festival at Lincoln Center in New York City. There Wynton hosts and performs in the Jazz for Young People concerts. This is one of the ways in which he hopes to spread a knowledge and love of jazz.

Accomplishments

1975 Soloist with New Orleans Philharmonic Orchestra.

1979-80 Played with Brooklyn Philharmonic Orchestra.

1980-81 Toured with the Jazz Messengers.

1981 Formed his own group.

1987 Became artistic director of jazz at Lincoln Center.

1994 Published the book *Sweet Swing Blues on the Road*.

1995 Hosted the TV series "Marsalis on Music."

Carmen McRae

Carmen's dream was to be a singer like Billie Holiday, but her parents did not want her to go into show business.

T he daughter of Jamaican immigrants, Carmen was raised in New York City. For five years, her parents paid for her to take piano lessons, hoping she would become a concert pianist. "I had no eyes for that," Carmen later recalled. "I'd keep sheet music of pop tunes hidden among the classical stuff, and when everyone was out of earshot I'd let go with the pops." Later, she was glad she had this grounding in classical music. She believed it helped her to become such a polished singer.

In 1939, when Carmen was seventeen, she won an amateur talent contest at the Apollo Theater in Harlem. Soon afterwards, she met her idol, Billie Holiday, who became a good friend. Carmen's dream was to be a singer like Billie, but her parents did not want her to go into show business. They insisted that she take a secretarial course and work in an office. She did so for several years while occasionally getting singing jobs in the evenings.

Carmen's first steady job as a soloist was for seventeen weeks in 1948 as a singer-pianist in a Chicago club. For the next four years, she stayed in Chicago, improving her act and gradually learning about show business. When Carmen returned to New York, she was a polished performer. She landed a job at Minton's Playhouse, playing the piano during the intermissions. Minton's was a Harlem club where many of the most famous jazz musicians played, and they quickly recognized Carmen's talent. Before long, she was performing there as a singer.

In 1953, Carmen made her first solo record. Her career took off in the next two years. She sang regularly at the Rainbow Grill in Manhattan and other stylish clubs, and she was in great demand at jazz festivals.

Personality Profile

Career: Singer and pianist.

Born: April 8, 1922, in New York City, New York, to Osmond and Evadne McRae.

Died: November 10, 1994, in Beverly Hills, California.

Education: Julia Richman High School.

Awards: Best New Female Singer in *Down Beat* magazine's poll, 1954; tied with Ella Fitzgerald for best female vocalist in *Metronome* magazine's readers' poll, 1955; Grammy nominations in 1971, 1977, 1984, 1987, 1988, 1990; Jazz Fellowship Award from the National Endowment for the Arts, 1994.

Meanwhile, she made many successful recordings. One of her biggest hits was the song "Take Five." Some people said Carmen's singing reminded them of Billie Holiday. Others saw a likeness to Sarah Vaughan. All saw a very great talent. She was particularly well known for her scat singing—the type of jazz that uses syllables instead of words.

Between 1961 and 1969, Carmen performed with her own trio. During this period, she recorded an album of Billie Holiday classics. Her later records ranged from *The Great American Songbook* (1972) to *Carmen Sings Monk* (1990) in which she sang lyrics to tunes composed by Thelonious Monk. She recorded almost two dozen albums during her career. Carmen also performed in television specials and in films, including the movies *Hotel* (1967) and *Jo Jo Dancer, Your Life Is Calling* (1986).

Carmen's talent was her interpretation of lyrics. Audiences hung on her words as though each song told a story. She has said that "the lyrics of a song I might decide to sing must have something that I can convince you with.... If I don't have something new to offer a song, well, I just won't sing it."

Accomplishments

1940 First singing engagements.

1948 Performed as soloist at a Chicago club.

1953 Released first solo album.

1967 Appeared in the movie *Hotel.*

1979 Television special, *Carmen McRae in Concert.*

1990 Released the album *Carmen Sings Monk.*

Nina Simone

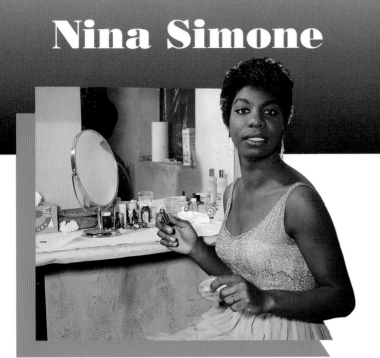

N ina was born Eunice Waymon, the sixth of eight children. Growing up in the 1940s in Tyron, North Carolina, she experienced the racism and poverty of the South. Nina could play the piano by ear at the age of three. When Nina was seven, her mother's boss offered to pay for piano lessons for Nina.

As Nina's piano playing improved, her teacher arranged for her to give piano recitals. Nina hated those concerts. The audience was always white, and there was sometimes a problem finding seats for her parents.

Recognizing Nina's special talent, her piano teacher set up the Eunice Waymon Fund to pay for her education. After each of Nina's performances, members of the audience were asked to contribute whatever they could. As a result, Nina studied at the famous Juilliard School of Music in New York City. But when she tried to complete her training at the Curtis Institute of Music in Philadelphia, she was not accepted.

"When I was a child, nobody was ever proud of me, and my people were never proud of themselves —or of anything they'd ever done. Well, that's different now. I'm proud of myself and I'm proud of my music."

Nina felt sure this rejection was because she was an African American. Nina's ambition was to be the first black concert pianist, and she did not want to give up her dream. She paid to have private lessons with a professor from the Curtis Institute. Meanwhile, she earned her living by playing the piano for children's singing lessons. When these stopped for the summer in 1954, she found a job as a pianist in an Atlantic City nightclub. This was the turning point in Nina's career.

When Nina sat down to play the piano her first night in Atlantic City, she found that she was expected to sing too. Nina had never thought she had a good voice. But the nightclub audience loved the way she sang. Instead of continuing as a classical piano player, Nina decided to follow a career in show business. She changed her name to Nina Simone to spare her mother's feelings, for her mother thought that pop music was sinful. She chose the name "Nina" because she had been called Niña, or little girl, when she was young. She added "Simone" because it sounded good with Nina.

During the following years, Nina became a regular performer in nightclubs and bars. As she became better known, she appeared on television and in the major concert halls. She was called the "High Priestess of Soul," because her singing was a blend of gospel music, jazz, classical, and popular tunes. Nobody before had ever sung quite the way Nina did.

Personality Profile

Career: Singer and songwriter.

Born: Eunice Waymon, February 21, 1935, in Tyron, North Carolina, to John and Mary Waymon.

Education: Allen High School for Girls; Juilliard School of Music.

Awards: Most Promising Singer of the Year, 1960; first woman to receive the Jazz Cultural Award, 1966; honored by Jazz at Home Club, New York City, as Woman of the Year, 1966; Female Jazz Singer of the Year, National Association of Television and Radio Announcers, 1967; Grammy nominations in 1967, 1970.

Nina was always outspoken. Once, she interrupted her performance to lecture a few noisy audience members on manners. In the 1960s, the civil rights movement gave Nina's energy a focus. She had always had a fierce pride in being African American, and now she began to speak out boldly. Some of the songs she wrote at this time were so outspoken that radio stations would not play them. Disenchanted with America, Nina moved to Barbados and then, in 1974, to West Africa. She has since settled in Europe, making her home in France.

Nina did not perform or record much during her traveling years, but she was back in the limelight in 1993 when she appeared in the film *Point of No Return*. That same year, her record *Single Woman* was a major hit. More than forty years after she first sang in public, Nina is still attracting new fans.

Accomplishments

1954 First performed as a singer, Midtown Bar, Atlantic City.

1958 Released *Little Girl Blue*.

1961 Visited Nigeria with American Society of African Culture.

1963 Toured with comedian Bill Cosby.

1965 First performance at Carnegie Hall, New York City.

1974 Moved to Liberia for two years.

1991 Published life story, *I Put a Spell on You*.

1993 Acted in the film *Point of No Return*.

Index

1 2 3 4 5 6 7 8 9 0 Printed in Canada 6 5 4 3 2 1 0 9 8 7